Baby
Animals

BABY AFRICAN ELEPHANTS

Martha E. H. Rustad

Raintree is an imprint of Capstone Global Library Limited, a company incorporated in England and Wales having its registered office at 264 Banbury Road, Oxford, OX2 7DY – Registered company number: 6695582

www.raintree.co.uk
myorders@raintree.co.uk

Edited by Alison Deering
Designed by Jennifer Bergstrom
Original illustrations © Capstone Global Library Limited 2022
Picture research by Tracy Cummins
Production by Tori Abraham
Originated by Capstone Global Library Ltd

978 1 3982 2377 6 (hardback)
978 1 3982 2378 3 (paperback)

British Library Cataloguing in Publication Data
A full catalogue record for this book is available from the British Library.

Acknowledgements
We would like to thank the following for permission to reproduce photographs: Alamy: MICHAEL CUTHBERT, 15; Shutterstock: Andre Klopper, back cover, Christin Winter, 17, Evelyn D. Harrison, 6, Four Oaks, 11, Henk Bogaard, 13, Mari Swanepoel, cover, Martin Mecnarowski, 5, matthieu Gallet, 9, Phillip Allaway, 19, Robby Holmwood, 7, Serg64, 20, slowmotiongli, 10, vesna cvorovic, 21.

Every effort has been made to contact copyright holders of material reproduced in this book. Any omissions will be rectified in subsequent printings if notice is given to the publisher.

All the internet addresses (URLs) given in this book were valid at the time of going to press. However, due to the dynamic nature of the internet, some addresses may have changed, or sites may have changed or ceased to exist since publication. While the author and publisher regret any inconvenience this may cause readers, no responsibility for any such changes can be accepted by either the author or the publisher.

Contents

A big baby 4

The herd 8

Eating, playing and communicating 12

Goodnight! 18

    Make your own elephant trunk 20

    Glossary 22

    Find out more 23

    Index 24

Words in **bold** are in the glossary.

A BIG BABY

Look! It's a new baby. It is an African elephant **calf**. It grew inside its mother's body for almost two years.

This baby is big. It weighs about 90 kilograms (200 pounds). Its skin is grey and it has fuzzy hair.

The calf tries to stand up. It needs help from its mother. She lifts it with her **trunk**.

Baby elephants drink milk from their mothers. The hungry baby sniffs under its mother. It opens its mouth and drinks. Babies need about 11 litres (19 pints) of milk every day.

THE HERD

Baby elephants live in a **herd**. Herds are made up of families. Aunts, sisters and cousins all live in the herd. They look after the calf together.

The baby learns to walk straight away. African elephants walk a long way every day. They look for plants to eat. They look for water to drink.

The herd slows down so the baby can keep up. The calf stays close to its mother.

A **clumsy** calf can trip on its trunk.

It learns how to hold its trunk up.

Other elephants show the baby how to suck up water. It learns to squirt water into its mouth. A calf sometimes sucks on its trunk. It's like a human baby sucking its thumb!

EATING, PLAYING AND COMMUNICATING

After six months, baby elephants start to eat other foods. They keep drinking milk for about two years.

The herd teaches the calf what to eat. African elephants eat grasses, leaves and fruit. They use their **tusks**. They dig for water and pull bark off trees.

tusk

Baby elephants are born with tiny tusks. They fall out after about one year. New tusks grow in. The calf's fuzzy hair also falls out after about a year.

Young elephants like to play. They twist their trunks together. They run around and roll over.

Baby elephants do not know how to swim. They learn from the herd. Elephants hold their trunks above the water to breathe.

Now it is time for a bath. A mother
sprays dust on her calf. Dust protects its
skin from insects and the heat of the Sun.

African elephants **communicate** with each other. They **trumpet** and sigh. They rumble and squeak. Young elephants learn what all the sounds mean.

Elephants can even send messages to other herds that are far away. An elephant's low rumble can travel many kilometres. Other herds sense these sounds as **vibrations** in the ground.

GOODNIGHT!

At night, the herd settles down. The baby elephant lies down to rest. Adults surround the calf. They keep it safe from **predators**. Adults sleep standing up.

Young elephants keep growing bigger until they are about 20 years old. They weigh up to 6 tonnes. That is the weight of about 5 or 6 horses!

Male elephants leave the herd at about 12 years old. Female elephants stay with the herd their whole lives.

MAKE YOUR OWN ELEPHANT TRUNK

A trunk is a helpful tool! Elephants use their trunks to say hello, to pick leaves from a tree and to suck up water. If you had a trunk, what would you do with it?

What you need

- tape or chalk
- paper
- pool noodles
- a friend
- a wide open place to play

What you do

1. Use tape or chalk to mark off a square on the ground. It should be in the centre of your play area. Make each side about as long as your arm.

2. Squish up pieces of paper into balls. Throw them around your play area, outside the square.

3. Hold one end of the pool noodle to your nose, just like an elephant's trunk. Use the other end of the noodle to push the paper balls into the square.

4. How many balls did you get in? How many did your friend get?

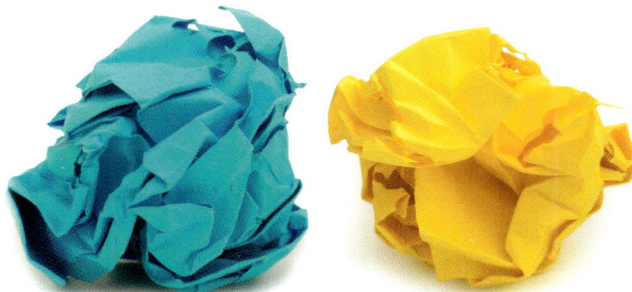

Glossary

calf young elephant

clumsy moving in a very awkward way

communicate use sounds or movements to explain something

herd group of animals that live together

predator animal that hunts other animals for food

trumpet make a loud sound like a trumpet

trunk very long nose of an elephant

tusk long tooth on an animal

vibration trembling motion

Find out more

Books

A Herd of Elephants (Animal Groups), Amy Kortuem (Raintree, 2020)

Elephant vs. Rhinoceros (Animal Rivals), Isabel Thomas (Raintree, 2018)

Websites

www.dkfindout.com/uk/animals-and-nature/elephants/
Learn more about elephants with DKFindout!

kids.nationalgeographic.com/animals/mammals/facts/african-elephant
Read some cool facts about elephants on the National Geographic website.

Index

appearance 4, 13

bathing 15

communication 16

diet 7, 8, 12
dust 15

hair 4, 13
herd 8, 9, 12, 14, 16,
     18, 19

milk 7, 12

playing 14
predators 18

size 4, 18
skin 4, 15
sleeping 18
sounds 16
swimming 14

travel 16
trunk 6, 10–11, 14
tusk 12, 13

walking 8, 9
water 8, 11, 12, 14